HOW TO HANDLE DEPRESSION:
Practical Guides To Overcome Depression And Improve Your Mental Health

Betty C. Elam

Table of content

CHAPTER 1

What is Depression??

Depression (major depressive disorder) is a frequent and significant medical ailment that adversely affects how you feel, the way you think, and how you behave. Thankfully, it is also curable. Depression creates feelings of despair and/or a lack of interest in activities you formerly liked. It may lead to several mental and physical difficulties and can limit your capacity to operate at work and home.

Depression is a mental condition that creates a continuous sensation of melancholy and lack of interest. Often termed major depressive disorder or clinical depression, it affects how you feel, thinks, and conduct yourself and may lead to many emotional and physical difficulties. You may have problems accomplishing basic day-to-day tasks, and occasionally you may feel as if life isn't worth living.

Truth about Depression

Throughout the last year, 8.4% of U.S. adults have experienced at least one severe depressive episode, which is defined as a sad mood or lack of interest in everyday activities lasting two weeks or longer. This percentage is significantly higher for females (10.5%), persons who are multiracial (15.9%), and people aged 18 to 25 (17%). Depression is frequent. Experts estimate that about 7% of individuals in the United States develop depression every year. More than 16% of U.S. adults — roughly 1 in 6 individuals — may suffer depression at some point in their lives.

Nevertheless, experts think that these estimations are lower than reality since many individuals don't seek medical care for symptoms of depression and don't acquire a diagnosis.

Around 4.4% of youngsters in the United States suffer from depression.

Depression is a very real and curable disorder. Yet misconceptions, misunderstandings, and stigma continue to be obstacles to therapy for many, and the consequences of untreated depression may be life-threatening. These are eight things everyone should know about depression and depressive illnesses.

8 Things You Should Know About Depression

1. Things Can Happen Without a Cause
2. It Has Several Causes
3. It Is More Than Grief/Sadness
4. It Can Happen to Kids
5. The Signs Of Depression
6. Risk factors
7. Complications
8. Prevention

- Depression Doesn't Always Have a "Good" Cause

Sometimes individuals get unhappy for what looks like a "good" reason—maybe they lost their job or a family member died away. But, with clinical depression, there doesn't necessarily have to be a cause for how you feel.

In reality, 16 million persons endure depression without encountering a terrible event or undergoing any form of life transition. This may lead to diminished sympathy from others, simply because they don't realize that depression can exist without a trigger or external stressor.

One reason for this is that depression has been related to an imbalance in the neurotransmitters that help control emotions. The assumption is that having too much or too little of these chemical messengers might cause (or contribute to) depression.

Consequently, the brain chemicals that are important for your mood may be out of balance, leading you to feel lousy even when everything in your life is going well.

- Several Causes Of Depression

The origin of depression isn't always totally understood, and many feel that this mental health problem is typically the consequence of a mix of events. The numerous causes of depression might include:

1. Genetics: Around 80 genetic variations have been found as being connected to depression. Several studies have revealed that when a parent has depression, a child's risk of depression is higher throughout adolescence and continuing into adulthood. This shows that genetics may play a role in this disease's development.

2. Hormones: Any fluctuation in the production or action of hormones—such as those associated with pregnancy, menstruation, menopause, or the thyroid—can contribute to depression. For example,

one research revealed that when premenopausal women had greater amounts of the hormone testosterone, they experienced more depressive symptoms.

3. Seasonal changes: Major depressive disorder with seasonal patterns (also known as seasonal affective disorder) is triggered by disruptions in the body's circadian rhythm at different times of the year. A change in seasons can also disrupt sleep, which can contribute to a depressed mood.

4. Stress and trauma: The death of a loved one, trauma, abuse, chronic stress, and substantial life changes (such as going through a divorce or losing a job) may precipitate depression. Researchers blame this on high quantities of the hormone cortisol that are released during stressful, traumatic situations. Cortisol impacts the neurotransmitter

serotonin and may produce depression.

5. Drug usage: Depression rates are also greater in those with a history of substance use. One reason for this is that the stigma of depression drives individuals to resort to drugs as a means of coping, or that depression leads to substance usage. Some ideas indicate that drug use leads to depression, or that both substance use and depression are the outcomes of a distinct underlying condition.

6. Biological differences. Individuals with depression seem to have physical alterations in their brains. The importance of these alterations is yet unknown, but may ultimately assist determine causes.

7. Brain chemistry. Neurotransmitters are naturally occurring brain chemicals that presumably have a role in depression. Current research shows that changes in the function and

action of these neurotransmitters and how they interact with neurocircuits essential in maintaining mood stability may play a crucial role in depression and its treatment.

Other probable reasons for depression include the existence of a physical health condition that typically co-occurs with this disease—such as cancer, diabetes, or Parkinson's—or using drugs that include depression as a side effect.

- Grief or Depression
1. Depression Is Distinct From Sorrow or Grief/Bereavement. The death of a loved one, the loss of a job, or the termination of a relationship are tough things for a person to face. It is typical for sentiments of melancholy or grief to arise in reaction to such events. People facing loss frequently would identify themselves as being "depressed."

Yet being sad is not the same as having depression. The mourning process is normal and unique to each person and includes some of the same elements of depression. Both sorrow and depression may include extreme sadness and withdrawal from customary activities. They are also distinct in crucial ways:

With sorrow, painful sensations come in waves, typically intermixed with happy recollections of the departed. With serious depression, mood and/or interest (pleasure) are lower for most of the two weeks.

With sorrow, self-esteem is frequently preserved. With serious depression, emotions of worthlessness and self-loathing are widespread.

In grieving, thoughts of death may occur while thinking about or daydreaming about "joining" the departed loved one. With serious depression, thoughts are concentrated on terminating one's life owing to feeling worthless or unworthy of living or being unable to deal with the agony of despair.

Sorrow and sadness may co-exist For some individuals, the loss of a loved one, losing a job, or being a victim of a physical attack or a big calamity may lead to sadness. When sorrow and depression co-occur, the grief is more profound and lasts longer than grief without depression.

Identifying between sorrow and depression is crucial and may aid individuals in receiving the assistance, support, or therapy they need.

- Children Are Not Immune to Depression

It's a fallacy that childhood is usually a joyous, carefree period. Although children may not suffer the same challenges as adults, such as work-related stress or financial demands, this doesn't imply that they can't get sad.

The Centers for Disease Control and Prevention (CDC) states that 4.4% of children aged 3 to 17 are diagnosed with depression or around 2.7 million in total.

14 Moreover, 73.8% of children with depression also have anxiety and 47.2% have behavior difficulties.

Childhood provides its own particular set of pressures, such as bullying (whether in person or online) and the quest for peer acceptance. Children might also feel anxious about academics, sports, body changes, or troubles occurring at home, including if their parents are going through a separation or divorce.

- Symptoms

While depression may strike just once throughout your life, individuals often experience several bouts. During these periods, symptoms occur most of the day, practically every day, and may include:

- ☐ Emotions of melancholy, tearfulness, emptiness, or despair
- ☐ Anger outbursts, impatience or annoyance, even over little concerns lack of interest or pleasure in most or all typical activities, such as sex sports, or hobbies,
- ☐ Sleep difficulties, include insomnia or sleeping too much
- ☐ Tiredness and lack of energy, so even minor things require additional effort
- ☐ Decreased appetite and weight loss or increased appetite for eating and weight gain
- ☐ Anxiety, agitation, or restlessness
- ☐ Slowed thinking, speaking, or bodily motions
- ☐ Emotions of worthlessness or remorse, fixating on previous failures or self-blame
- ☐ Difficulty thinking, focusing, making judgments, and remembering things

☐ Frequent or repeated thoughts of death, suicidal thoughts, suicide attempts, or suicide
☐ Unexplained bodily concerns, such as back pain or headaches

For many persons with depression, symptoms are normally often severe enough to produce visible issues in day-to-day activities, such as job, school, social activities, or relationships with others. Some individuals may feel generally unpleasant or depressed without actually understanding why.

Depressive symptoms in children and teenagers
Typical indications and symptoms of depression in adolescents and teens are similar to those of adults, although there might be significant distinctions.

In younger children, signs of depression may include sorrow, irritability, clinginess, concern, aches, pains, refusing to go to school, or being underweight.

In teens, symptoms may include sadness, irritability, feeling negative and worthless, anger, poor performance or poor attendance at school, feeling misunderstood and extremely sensitive, using recreational drugs or alcohol, eating or sleeping too much, self-harm, loss of interest in normal activities, and avoidance of social interaction.

Depressive symptoms in elderly individuals
Depression is not a natural aspect of getting older, and it should never be treated lightly. Regrettably, depression commonly remains undetected and untreated in older individuals, and they may feel hesitant to seek treatment.
Signs of depression may be different or less visible in older persons, such as:

☐ Memory problems or personality changes
☐ Physical pains or discomfort
☐ Fatigue, lack of appetite, sleep issues, or loss of desire for sex — not caused by a medical condition or medicine
☐ Frequently desiring to remain at home, rather than going out to mingle or doing new activities
☐ Suicidal thoughts or sentiments, particularly among elderly males

- Risk factors

Depression commonly starts in the teens, 20s, or 30s, although it may strike at any age. More women than males are diagnosed with depression, however, this may be attributable in part because women are more willing to seek therapy.

Factors that appear to enhance the likelihood of developing or causing depression include:

- ☐ Some personality qualities, such as poor self-esteem and being excessively reliant, self-critical, or pessimistic
- ☐ Painful or stressful situations, such as physical or sexual abuse, the death or loss of a loved one, a challenging relationship, or financial troubles
- ☐ Blood relations with a history of depression, bipolar illness, alcoholism, or suicide
- ☐ Being homosexual, gay, bisexual, or transgender, or having variances in the development of genital organs that aren't unmistakably male or female (intersex) in an unsupportive context
- ☐ History of various mental health illnesses, such as anxiety disorder, eating disorders, or post-traumatic stress disorder
- ☐ Misuse of alcohol or recreational drugs
- ☐ Severe or chronic sickness, including cancer, stroke, chronic pain, or heart disease

Some drugs, such as certain high blood pressure meds or sleeping pills (speak to your doctor before quitting any prescription) (talk to your doctor before stopping any medication)

- Complications

Depression is a severe condition that may take a horrible toll on you and your family. Depression frequently grows worse if it isn't addressed, resulting in emotional, behavioral, and physiological issues that influence every part of your life.

Examples of problems related to depression include:

- ☐ Excess weight or obesity, which may contribute to heart disease and diabetes
- ☐ Pain or physical sickness
- ☐ Alcohol or drug misuse
- ☐ Anxiety, panic disorder, or social phobia

- ☐ Family disputes, interpersonal troubles, and job or school challenges
- ☐ Social isolation\s Suicidal emotions, suicide attempts, or suicide
- ☐ Self-mutilation, such as cutting
- ☐ Premature death from medical disorders

- • Prevention

There's no proven method to avoid depression. But, these measures may assist.

1. Take efforts to manage stress, enhance your resilience, and raise your self-esteem.
2. Reach out to family and friends, particularly in times of crisis, to help you weather hard situations.
3. Seek therapy at the first indication of a problem to help prevent depression from worsening.

4. Consider seeking long-term maintenance therapy to help avoid a return of symptoms.

CHAPTER 2

WHAT ARE THE TYPES OF DEPRESSION?

The American Psychiatric Association's Diagnostic Statistical Manual of Mental Disorders, Fifth Edition (DSM-5) includes depressive illnesses as the following:

Clinical depression (major depressive disorder): A diagnosis of the major depressive disorder indicates you've felt sad, down, or worthless most days for at least two weeks while also experiencing additional symptoms such as sleep difficulties, lack of interest in activities, or change in food. This is the most severe kind of depression and one of the most frequent sorts.

Persistent depressive disorder (PDD): Persistent depressive disorder is mild to moderate depression that lasts for at least two years. The symptoms are less severe than a major depressive disorder. Healthcare practitioners used to term PDD dysthymia.

Disruptive mood dysregulation disorder (DMDD): DMDD causes persistent, high irritation and frequent angry outbursts in youngsters. Symptoms commonly develop around the age of 10.

Premenstrual dysphoric disorder (PMDD): In PMDD, you experience premenstrual syndrome (PMS) symptoms associated with mood symptoms, such as severe irritability, anxiety, or sadness. These symptoms lessen within a few days after your period begins, but they might be severe enough to interfere with your life.

Depressive disorder owing to another medical condition: Several medical problems might induce changes in your body that cause depression. Examples include hypothyroidism, heart disease, Parkinson's disease, and cancer. If you're able to cure the underlying problem, depression generally improves as well.

There are additional distinct kinds of major depressive illness, including:

Seasonal affective disorder (seasonal depression): This is a sort of major depressive illness that normally occurs throughout the autumn and winter and goes away during the spring and summer.

Prenatal depression and postpartum depression: Prenatal depression is depression that occurs during pregnancy. Postpartum depression is depression that begins within four weeks after having a baby. The DSM refers to them as "major depressive disorder (MDD) with peripartum onset."

Atypical depression: Symptoms of this ailment, also known as the major depressive disorder with atypical characteristics, differ somewhat from "typical" depression. The key distinction is a brief mood enhancement in reaction to pleasant occurrences (mood reactivity) (mood reactivity). Some major symptoms include increased hunger and rejection sensitivity.

Individuals with bipolar illness can have bouts of depression in addition to manic or hypomanic episodes.

CHAPTER 3

How Is Depression Treated?

Depression is among the most curable mental diseases. Between 80% and 90% percent of persons with depression ultimately react effectively to therapy. Virtually all people obtain some alleviation from their symptoms.

Before a diagnosis or therapy, a health practitioner should do a full diagnostic assessment, including an interview and a physical examination. In rare situations, a blood test could be done to make sure the depression is not related to a medical issue like a thyroid problem or a vitamin deficiency (reversing the medical reason would ease the depression-like symptoms) (reversing the medical cause would alleviate the depression-like symptoms). The examination will identify specific symptoms and investigate medical and family histories as well as cultural and environmental variables to arrive at a diagnosis and create a course of action.

- MEDICATION

Brain chemistry may contribute to an individual's depression and may play into their therapy. For this reason, antidepressants could be recommended to assist change one's brain chemistry. These drugs are not sedatives, "uppers" or tranquilizers. They are not habit-forming. Usually, antidepressant drugs have a little stimulating impact on those not suffering from depression.

Antidepressants may offer some relief during the first week or two of treatment although complete effects may not be apparent for two to three months. If a patient experiences little or no improvement after many weeks, his or her psychiatrist may modify the amount of the drug or add or replace another antidepressant. In certain cases, different psychotropic medicines may be beneficial. It is crucial to let your doctor know if a drug does not work or if you encounter negative effects.

Psychiatrists frequently suggest that patients continue to take medication for six or more months after the symptoms have improved. Longer-term maintenance therapy may be implied to lower the likelihood of subsequent episodes for select patients at high risk.

- PSYCHOTHERAPY

Psychotherapy, or "talk therapy," is occasionally used alone for the treatment of mild depression; for moderate to severe depression, psychotherapy is generally used combined with antidepressant medicines. Cognitive behavioral therapy (CBT) has been demonstrated to be useful in treating depression. CBT is a kind of treatment focusing on the issue resolution in the present. CBT assists a person to detect distorted/negative thinking to modify ideas and actions to react to situations more positively.

Psychotherapy may include merely the person, but it may include others. For example, family or couples counseling may assist address concerns within these intimate connections. Group therapy brings individuals with similar conditions together in a supportive setting, and may allow the participant to understand how others manage in similar circumstances.

Depending on the severity of the depression, therapy might take a few weeks or much more. In many situations, considerable progress may be achieved after 10 to 15 sessions.

- ELECTROCONVULSIVE TREATMENT (ECT)\sECT is a medical therapy that has been most typically reserved for patients with severe serious depression who have not responded to previous therapies. It includes a short electrical stimulation of the brain while the patient is under anesthesia. A patient normally undergoes ECT two to three times a week for a total of six to 12 sessions. It is normally supervised by a team of experienced medical experts comprising a psychiatrist, an anesthesiologist, and a nurse or physician assistant. ECT has been utilized since the 1940s, and many years of study have led to considerable advances and the acknowledgment of its usefulness as a mainstream rather than a "last resort" therapy.

- SELF-HELP AND COPING

There are a lot of things individuals may take to assist minimize the symptoms of depression. For many individuals, daily exercise helps develop happy emotions and enhances mood. Obtaining adequate quality sleep regularly, eating a nutritious diet, and avoiding alcohol (a depressive) may also help minimize symptoms of depression.

Depression is a genuine condition and assistance is available. With appropriate diagnosis and therapy, the great majority of persons with depression will overcome it. If you are suffering from signs of depression, the first step is to consult your family physician or psychiatrist. Speak about your issues and seek a comprehensive review. This is a start to addressing your mental health requirements.